Weekend Walks by the Thames

Short Scenic Strolls For All Ages
in Berkshire and Oxfordshire

John Prior

Nine Peas
Publishing

Published by Nine Peas Publishing

First published 2021

© John Prior 2021

ISBN 978-0-9929688-3-0

Designed by Chris Preston

Typeset by Chris Preston

Printed by Press to Print Reading Ltd

Weekend Walks
by the Thames

Short Scenic Strolls For All Ages
in Berkshire and Oxfordshire

PUBLISHER'S NOTE
Whilst great care has been taken to provide information about
the route, facilities and public transport for each walk that is accurate at
the time of publication, the publisher cannot be held responsible for
any inaccuracies or changes. However, feedback and updated
information from readers is welcomed, for any future editions
(email:ninepeaspublishing@btinternet.com). The sketch maps that
accompany the walks show only the main paths, roads and buildings
referred to in the route notes; Ordnance Survey maps provide
fuller information. All distances are approximate.

*Please note that this book was written during the coronavirus pandemic,
when the availability of public transport and facilities such as cafes
and shops was affected. Therefore checks for any future changes are
recommended, using web-sites where available.*

The cover photographs, clockwise from top left, are :
Spring Cottages, Sonning (walk 9)
Culham Lock life saver (walk 11)
Boathouse at Cleeve (walk 10)
Mute Swan (all walks!)
Thames Path sign, Shiplake (walk 8)
Whitchurch Bridge, Pangbourne (walk 6)

Symbols used on maps

Walk Start	⬤
Toilets	🚹🚺
Café/Pub/Shop	☕
Playground	🎠
Viewpoint	☀
Railway Station	⇌

Contents

DEDICATION
To my wife Anne, daughters Jo, Cathy and Sarah
and grandchildren Ben, Josh, Hannah, Ethan and Dylan.

ACKNOWLEDGEMENT and THANKS
To Chris for his patience and professionalism in
turning my typescript into this book.

Introduction

As the River Thames meanders its way for 215 miles from the Cotswolds to the North Sea, many of the most beautiful reaches are to be found in Berkshire and Oxfordshire. The Thames Path National Trail means that these are easily accessible for walkers. These 12 circular walks explore the river that inspired those classic books *The Wind in the Willows* by Kenneth Grahame and *Three Men in a Boat* by Jerome K Jerome.

Each route is no more than 3 miles long, mainly level, and incorporates places of interest and stops for refreshments or a picnic. Most also include a children's playground, or there is one nearby. The starting points have been chosen for easy car parking and/or access by public transport. Numbers within the route descriptions link to facts and figures about the places passed.

The walks will suit anyone who wants some exercise for an hour or so in interesting surroundings. So pick a route and head off to discover the glorious Thames Valley. Despite the title, it doesn't *have* to be at a weekend!

2021 marks two notable anniversaries for the Thames – 25 years since the establishment of the Thames Path and 250 years since the founding of the Thames Navigation Commissioners, who managed the river before the Thames Conservancy. The Berkshire Record Office recently completed a catalogue of their unique, unbroken records of these organisations.

The author

For over 40 years I've lived near the Thames in Pangbourne, where my wife Anne and I brought up our three daughters. At weekends we were keen to explore the local area but any walk had to be child-friendly – not too long and, if possible, including a playground and an ice-cream!

Our first collection of family walks was published in *Weekend Walks West of Reading* and this was followed by *Weekend Walks South of Oxford*. These proved popular so this is a third collection, focussing on the River Thames. Being 'senior citizens' with five grandchildren, these walks were again chosen with both the young and the not-so-young in mind!

Walk Locations

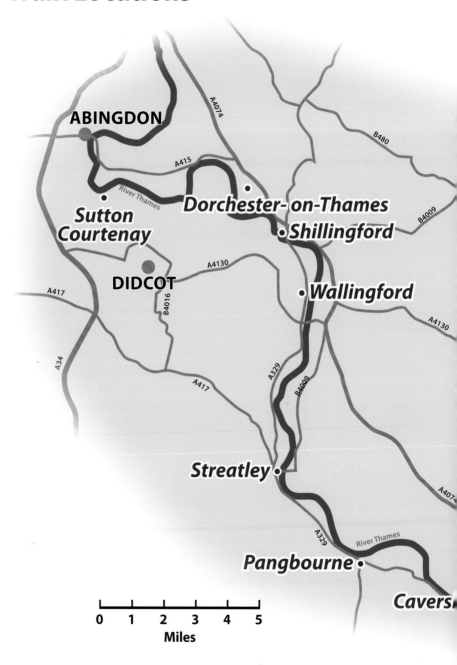

Explore this busy part of the Thames, to see birds, boats and bridges.

START/PARKING: Rivermead Leisure Complex car park (pay and display, 3 hours free), Richfield Avenue off Caversham Road (A4155), Reading (Nat Grid Ref 41/705745, Postcode RG1 8EQ). Alternative parking nearby at Thames Side Promenade, Richfield Avenue (pay and display Mon - Fri, 2 hours free)
PUBLIC TRANSPORT: Reading Buses routes 22, 24 and 27/29 and Thames Travel buses X39/X40 Reading to Oxford
DISTANCE: 2 miles (3¼ km) or 2¾ miles (4½ km)
REFRESHMENTS: Kiosk at Reading Rowing Club, Thames Side Promenade (Summer); Crowne Plaza Hotel Riverside Terrace; The Griffin pub, Church Road; Tea Kiosk in Caversham Court Gardens (March to October, see www.theteakiosk.org.uk)
PUBLIC TOILETS: Rivermead Leisure Complex, Caversham Court Gardens, Christchurch Meadows (near children's playground)
PATHS: Pavements and surfaced riverside paths (may be flooded when the Thames is high)
CHILDREN'S PLAYGROUND: Rivermead and Christchurch Meadows

THE ROUTES: Near the Rivermead car park is a children's playground suitable for primary and pre-school children. Take the path to the left of here through a shady area with seats towards the Thames. Turn right to join the riverside path; on the opposite bank are Caversham Court Gardens. There are usually large flocks of (hungry!) swans, geese and gulls along here and by the Reading Rowing Club and Caversham Pier. Just beyond the Crowne Plaza Hotel, take the path to the right to cross Caversham Bridge ❶; there are fine views of the river upstream. Continue past a row of shops to a road junction.

To visit the beautiful gardens of nearby Caversham Court ❷, turn left into Church Road and after passing The Griffin pub, the gated entrance to the gardens is by a bend in the road. Just inside is an information panel showing the main features of the gardens, whose shady, terraced lawns slope down from attractive St Peter's parish church to the river. The footprint of the old house is shown by a brick pattern, with a panel by the path up to the church explaining this and the development of the house. After exploring the gardens, retrace your steps along Church Road to the junction and carefully cross Bridge Street at the traffic lights. Turn right towards the bridge then left into Promenade Road. This leads to Christchurch Meadows, with the Reading University Boat Club on the left and the riverside path ahead. This passes Fry's Island, with boathouses and moorings, opposite which is an information board by the path. There is a children's playground and paddling pool just beyond Christchurch Bridge ❸. For the shorter walk, cross this footbridge then turn right down steps to join the riverside path. Follow this under Caversham Bridge and past Reading Rowing Club to the start of the walk.

For the longer walk, visiting Caversham Lock, continue along the riverside path under Reading Bridge ❹. Just before some riverside housing, where the main path curves left, take a path to the right over short footbridges and then follow a shady path along the edge of View Island. This leads over a foaming weir to Caversham Lock. After crossing the lock, turn right to join the riverside path. This leads under Reading Bridge to the end of

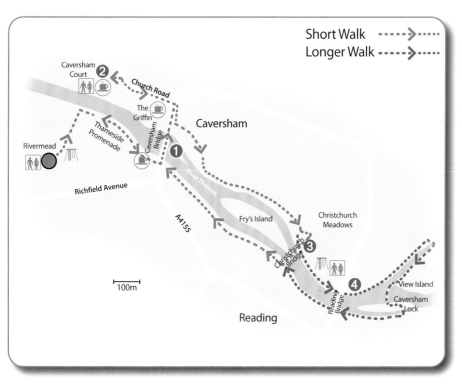

Christchurch Bridge, then past riverside properties towards Caversham Bridge. Continue under the bridge past Reading Rowing Club to the start of the walk.

Facts and Figures

❶ Caversham Bridge was constructed in 1924-26. Near the Reading end of the bridge is an embossed metal plaque giving information about the river crossings here since the 13th century. For 200m upstream and downstream of the bridge, the river is designated as a swan sanctuary.

❷ The gardens were originally part of the grounds surrounding Caversham Rectory, dating back to the 12th century. The Rectory was renamed Caversham Court in 1916 and in the 1930s, by then in decline, it was bought by Reading Corporation who demolished it and opened the gardens to the public. These were refurbished in 2008-09 and have since won several awards, with support from the Friends of Caversham Court Gardens (www.fccg.org.uk).

❸ Christchurch Bridge for pedestrians and cyclists was opened in 2015. The striking design uses 14 pairs of cables supported by a 50 tonne white mast. The name for the Meadows (and now the bridge) results from them being given to Christchurch College, Oxford by Henry VIII in 1539.

❹ Reading Bridge was completed in 1923, to provide a road crossing before the old Caversham Bridge was replaced.

Christchurch Bridge

Caversham Bridge

WALK TWO : COOKHAM

A riverside stroll from a pretty village associated with artist Stanley Spencer.

START/PARKING: National Trust car park (pay and display but free to NT members) at Cookham Moor on the B4447 west of Cookham (Nat Grid Ref 41/895854, Postcode SL6 9QQ). Alternative (limited) parking in Cookham village centre
PUBLIC TRANSPORT: Cookham rail station, just under ½ mile from the start. Arriva bus route 37 from Maidenhead to High Wycombe, Mon – Sat
DISTANCE: 1¾ miles (2¾ km)
REFRESHMENTS: The Crown, Bel and the Dragon and Kings Arms pubs; Teapot tea shop and Mr Cooper's Coffee House in High St.
PUBLIC TOILETS: Sutton Road car park (near corner High St/Sutton Rd)
PATHS: Level footpaths and pavements. Some paths are liable to be muddy after wet weather (and may be flooded when the Thames is high)
CHILDREN'S PLAYGROUND: None known

THE ROUTE: From the car park, follow the grassy footpath across Cookham Moor towards the village, to reach The Crown pub on the left. From here, go ahead along the High Street with its attractive mix of old buildings. On the right these include a house called 'Fernlea', with a blue plaque commemorating artist Stanley Spencer ❶ and the 17th century Kings Arms. Further along is the 15th century Bel and the Dragon inn. On the corner at the junction is the former Methodist Chapel, now the Stanley Spencer Gallery. Turn left here, passing the Tarry Stone ❷ in front of a seat on the corner of Odney Lane. A short distance beyond, turn left into Church Gate and then right into the churchyard of Holy Trinity ❸. Follow the path, keeping left of the church, to reach the River Thames. Cookham Bridge can be seen downstream from here.

Turn left and follow the tarmac footpath across Bell Rope Meadow (a former ropewalk, see information panel), where there are plenty of benches for a pause or a picnic. The path leads past Cookham Reach Sailing Club and into Marsh Meadow. Follow the riverside path for about half a mile, with glorious views of the Thames upstream and the Chilterns beyond. Just before a metal kissing gate, turn left along a grassy path towards woods and a railway bridge (for the Marlow branch line). Before reaching this bridge, just after the path crosses a small stream (The Strand), turn left to join a shady track running parallel to this stream. Follow this track along the stream, with views of the Thames and Cookham Bridge to the left, to reach a small footbridge by the car park and the start of the walk.

"Believe me, my young friend, there is nothing – absolutely nothing – half so much worth doing as simply messing about in boats" - Ratty to Mole in 'The Wind in the Willows'.

Kenneth Grahame spent part of his life at nearby Cookham Dean and the local woods and river are thought to be the inspiration for his classic book.

Facts and Figures

❶ Sir Stanley Spencer (1891-1959) is one of the most admired artists of the 20th century. He spent much of his life in Cookham and the village features in many of his paintings, which often depict biblical scenes. The Stanley Spencer Gallery houses an important collection of his works; it is open daily from April to October and Thu-Sun in winter (www.stanleyspencer.org.uk). He and his first wife Hilda are buried in the churchyard of Holy Trinity.

❷ The Tarry Stone is a large sarsen stone used as a boundary marker and at which the annual village sports were held before 1505. It has been moved to various locations but is now thought to be in its original position.

❸ Holy Trinity Church is mostly 13th century but the Lady Chapel dates back to Norman times. Inside there is a copy of Spencer's *The Last Supper* and some colourful stained glass windows. The simple headstone of Sir Stanley Spencer's grave is close to the path through the churchyard, on the left about halfway between the entrance and the church.

Holy Trinity

Can you spot Stanley Spencer?

Blue Plaque at Fernlea

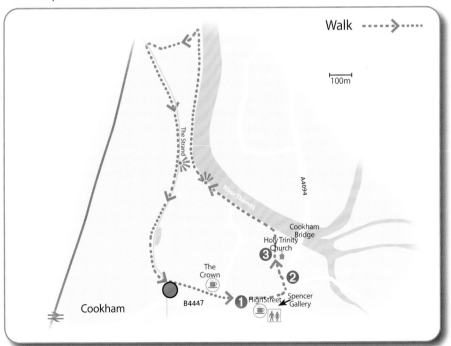

Walk ·····▷·····

100m

The Strand

River Thames

A4094

Cookham Bridge

Holy Trinity Church

③

②

The Crown

① High Street

Spencer Gallery

Cookham

B4447

From this picturesque village, with its magnificent Abbey, across water meadows to a busy lock. The walk may be extended to take in glorious views over the Thames Valley.

START/PARKING: Dorchester lies off the A4074, 10 miles SE of Oxford. The walk starts in Bridge End, close to Dorchester Bridge, where there is a small car park and roadside parking (Nat Grid Ref 41/578939, Postcode OX10 7JP)

PUBLIC TRANSPORT: Thames Travel buses X38/X39/X40 Oxford-Wallingford-Reading/Henley stop on the Dorchester by-pass, from where a short walk through the village leads to Bridge End

DISTANCE: 2 miles (3¼ km) or 3 miles (4¾ km)

REFRESHMENTS: Abbey Tea Room (open Wed to Sun and BH afternoons from Easter to September), the Fleur de Lys (FDL), George and White Hart pubs, Lily's Tea Room (closed Tues) and Co-op store (open daily) - all in the High Street

PUBLIC TOILETS: In Bridge End

PATHS: Village roads and footpaths, liable to be muddy after wet weather (and riverside path flooded when the Thames is high). The optional extension involves a steep climb

CHILDREN'S PLAYGROUND: Recreation Ground off Drayton Road at the northern end of High Street

THE ROUTES: From the start, go along Bridge End, passing the Church of St Birinus on the left, to a small village green. Keep straight ahead, with the green on your left, and at the far end of a terrace of cottages on the right, take a narrow footpath to the right that leads to a lane by a thatched cottage. Turn left here to pass through a metal gate to a footpath along a field edge. The steep slopes of Wittenham Clumps ❶ lie ahead and the low grassy mounds of the Dyke Hills ❷ stretch away to the right. After passing a brick WW2 pill box, follow the grassy path ahead. Shortly, the meandering River Thame appears on the left, just before it enters the Thames. Turn right here on to the Thames Path. Wittenham Woods slope down to the opposite bank before the path curves right to a footbridge downstream of Day's Lock ❸.

This footbridge crosses to Lock House Island, and a wider bridge beyond gives views of the weir and pool. This leads to the tiny village of Little Wittenham, from where there is the option of extending the walk by about a mile to see glorious views (see * on page 12).

If you want to see the lock, follow the path under the footbridge. By the lock, turn right through a gate and cross a field to reach a gate by a Dorchester information panel. Alternatively, if you have crossed the bridge, at the Dorchester end pass through a metal gate to join a straight path bearing away from the river. This leads to a gate by a Dorchester information panel. The path then runs between fences and hedges into the undulating land of the Dyke Hills, turning right to run alongside their northern embankment. Half way along this, bear left across a field towards Dorchester.

At the village, take the path ahead to reach a lane. Turn left here and at the edge of allotments on the right, turn right along a path. This leads through the allotments, passing cottages on the left. After leaving the allotments, a narrow walled path emerges by a row of thatched cottages where a turn to the left leads to the High Street with its Abbey, fine houses, pretty cottages and former coaching inns. One of these, the Fleur de Lys (FDL), is on the left here and the grounds of the Abbey ❹ are

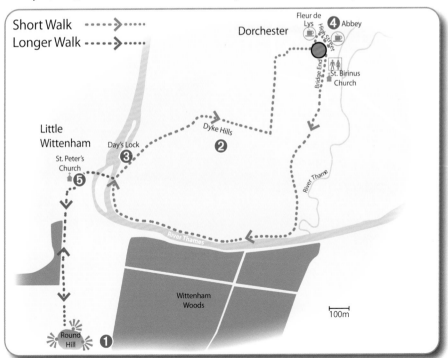

opposite. This beautiful building is well worth visiting, with a museum and tea room in the former Abbey guest house nearby. Bridge End and the start of the walk is close by to the right.

* To visit Round Hill, first cross the bridges at Lock House Island to join a lane into Little Wittenham. This leads to St Peter's church **❺** on the right, with shady seats by the churchyard wall. Go through the wooden gate opposite the church and ahead at the fork in the paths. After a metal gate, a broad grassy track climbs steeply through a meadow, colourful with wild flowers in summer. This leads to the summit of Round Hill at 390 ft (120m), from where there are panoramic views over Oxfordshire; a metal viewpoint plaque indicates the places that may be seen. Walking around the small hilltop wood gives further views to the south and of nearby Castle Hill. After admiring the views, re-trace your steps down the hill to the bridges near Day's Lock.

"It is very old and it was very strong and great once. Now it sits aside from the stirring world, and nods and dreams", Jerome K Jerome describing Dorchester in Chapter XVIII of 'Three Men in a Boat'

High Street

Bridge near Day's Lock

Facts and Figures

❶ The twin Sinodun Hills (Round Hill and Castle Hill) are more commonly known as Wittenham Clumps. Crowned by distinctive clumps of trees, mainly beech, they afford wide views over the surrounding countryside. Castle Hill is the site of an Iron Age hillfort with banks and ditches. The hills are part of Little Wittenham Nature Reserve, 250 acres of grassland and woodland managed by the Earth Trust charity (www.earthtrust.org.uk).

❷ The earthworks of the Dyke Hills are the remains of Iron Age defences. These consisted of two banks and a ditch between the rivers Thames and Thame, protecting a settlement. At the eastern end there are also five barrows, thought to be Bronze Age burial sites.

❸ The first pound lock was built here in 1789 and named after the Days, a local family. It became famous as the site of the World Pooh Sticks Championships, held annually for some 35 years until 2015. Winnie the Pooh's game was played from the bridge leading to Little Wittenham, raising funds for the RNLI.

❹ The Abbey church of St Peter and St Paul was established as an Augustinian monastery in the mid-12th century on the site of a Saxon cathedral. Among the many treasures are a Norman decorated font, medieval stone effigies and a stained glass window of the Tree of Jesse (www.dorchester-abbey.org.uk).

❺ The oldest part of St Peter's is the 14th century tower, with a staircase turret on the side. Inside there are a number of interesting memorial brasses from the 15th century and a 17th century alabaster monument to Sir William Dunch and his family.

A walk exploring more of Dorchester and the neighbouring hamlet of Overy is given in *Weekend Walks South of Oxford*

Discover a reach of the river that is full of interest, with foaming weirs, a picturesque mill and an elegant ornamental temple.

START/PARKING: Ferry Lane, Aston reached down Aston Lane off the A4130 at Remenham Hill, about 1½ miles east of Henley-on-Thames (NGR 41/787845, Postcode RG9 3DH). There is roadside parking at the riverside end of the lane. Alternatively, the nearby Flower Pot Hotel has a car park for customers
PUBLIC TRANSPORT: Arriva bus routes 800/850 Reading – Henley- High Wycombe serve Mill End, Hambleden close to the route
DISTANCE: 3 miles (4¾ km)
REFRESHMENTS: Flower Pot Hotel (www.brakspear.co.uk), open lunchtimes and evenings Mon-Fri, 12 to 9pm Sat and lunchtime Sun
PUBLIC TOILETS: Mill End car park, Hambleden (accessed via Hambleden Lock) and toilets at the Flower Pot Hotel for customers
PATHS: Lanes and footpaths, mainly level but one short uphill stretch; paths liable to be muddy after wet weather (and riverside path flooded when the Thames is high)
CHILDREN'S PLAYGROUND: None on walk, nearest is at Mill Meadows Henley-on-Thames

THE ROUTE: At the end of Ferry Lane turn left to join the riverside path, which has plenty of space for picnics and benches from which to enjoy views of the river and the wooded Chilterns beyond. After about ½ mile the path reaches Hambleden Lock. A path leads across the lock gates and bridges over four weirs to picturesque Hambleden Mill ❶; a diversion over these foaming waterfalls is well worth it. To continue the walk, rejoin the riverside path at the lock. Shortly, a white mansion surrounded by magnificent trees is seen on the opposite bank – this is Greenlands ❷. Then, as the river curves, the town of Henley comes into view dominated by the tower of its parish church. Just before wooded Temple Island ❸, look out for the metal plaque on the riverbank marking the start of the straight regatta course.

About ¼ mile beyond the island, leave the riverside path by turning left through a gate then along a path by a wall leading to Remenham village. Just beyond the flint-faced church of St Nicholas, turn left at the T junction then opposite the Old School House turn right into Remenham Church

Lane. Follow this lane uphill through the trees and at the end of the wood, by a metal gate, turn left to join a footpath across the fields. Go ahead along this path from which there are wide views over the Thames Valley. After about ¾ mile, ignore a path going downhill to the left and go through a gate then downhill across a field to reach Aston Lane. The Flower Pot Hotel is a short distance to the left, with Ferry Lane and the start of the walk just beyond.

"From Medmenham to sweet Hambleden Lock the river is full of peaceful beauty…", Chapter XIII of 'Three Men in a Boat' by Jerome K Jerome

A riverside walk upstream from nearby Henley-on-Thames is given in *Weekend Walks South of Oxford*

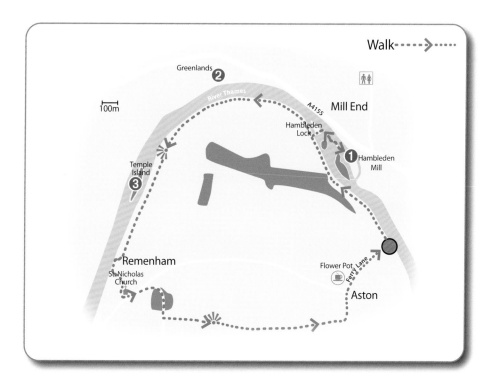

Facts and Figures

❶ A mill here was mentioned in the Domesday Book of 1086. The taller part of the mill dates from the late 1700s and the lower part along the waterfront is a 19th century addition. The attractive weather-boarded building was converted to apartments in the 1970s.

❷ This grand 19th century house is the former home of William Henry Smith, son of the founder of W H Smiths newsagents. It is now the Henley Business School, part of the University of Reading.

❸ Temple Island is named after a folly built in 1771 as a fishing lodge for nearby Fawley Court. The Island marks the start of the 2112m course of the Henley Royal Regatta and is leased by the regatta. The meadows on the Berkshire bank belong to Remenham Farm and are used for events, notably corporate hospitality during regatta week.

Hambleden Mill

Temple Island - Regatta Course mark

Temple Island

Explore this attractive village with an intriguing history, where wooded islands divide the Thames.

START/PARKING: Car park (free) at the far end of High Street, Hurley off the A4130 about 4 miles east of Henley and 1½ miles west of the A404 junction (Nat Grid Ref 41/825840, Postcode SL6 5NB). Roadside parking also available in High Street
PUBLIC TRANSPORT: Thames Valley bus route 239 Henley to Maidenhead, Mon/Wed/Fri
DISTANCE: 1¾ miles (2¾ km)
REFRESHMENTS: Rising Sun pub (www.risingsunhurley.co.uk), Olde Bell Inn (www.theoldebell.co.uk), Village Shop (open to 5pm Mon-Fri and to 4pm Sun) and tea shop at Hurley Lock (Tues-Sun in summer)
PUBLIC TOILETS: Lock Island (between the Upper Horse Bridge and Lock) and toilets at the Rising Sun and Olde Bell Inn for customers
PATHS: Village roads, footpaths and a farm track; level apart from two steep footbridges. The riverside paths may be flooded when the Thames is high.
CHILDREN'S PLAYGROUND: Henley Road (A4130), just west of the junction with High Street, Hurley

THE ROUTE: At the car park entrance, turn left on a tarmac path, passing on your right a small triangular green with a large cedar in the middle. Go past the gate for Tithecote Manor and take the narrow path ahead. This leads to the riverside and a footbridge - the Upper Horse Bridge. Hurley Weir is a short distance to the left here. To continue the walk, cross the bridge and follow the path along Lock Island towards picturesque Hurley Lock ❶. There are benches to sit and watch the river activity – you may spot a classic wooden launch from Freebody's boatyard, just downstream. Close by the lock, a tree commemorates a river journey from here made by the Queen in 1974. Continue along the island past picnic benches to reach another footbridge – the Lower Horse Bridge.

Follow the riverside path, with a view of Temple footbridge a short distance downstream. Before reaching this, take a footpath to the right alongside a wooden fence and then at a kissing gate turn right again to join a stony track through fields. Where a footpath leaves to the right go through a kissing gate and immediately bear left to follow a narrow footpath between hedges. At a tarmac road, take the path straight ahead. This leads back to Hurley, by the ancient Olde Bell Inn ❷ – look for the bell by the porch. Turn right here along the High Street, which is full of interest. On the left is the entrance to Hurley Manor, a blue plaque commemorating its role as a secret wartime US radio station. Nearby on the right are 17th century almshouses and Church House dating from 1494 then further along on the left, just past the Village Shop, the medieval chalk and flint Monks Barn. At the far end of High Street are the remains of the Benedictine Priory, notably the parish church of St Mary the Virgin ❸ - well worth a visit. The start of the walk is close by.

"By Hurley Weir . . . . . . I could stay a month without having sufficient time to drink in all the beauty of the scene", Chapter XIII of 'Three Men in a Boat' by Jerome K Jerome

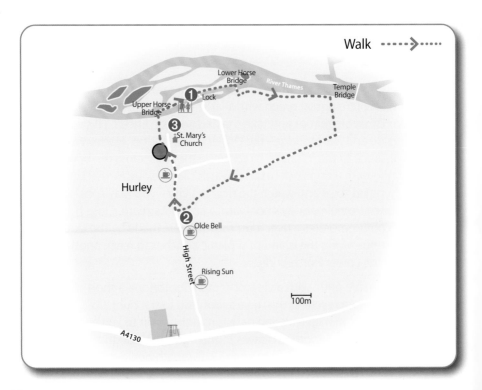

Facts and Figures

❶ The pound lock was first built in 1773, replacing a flash lock near the weir a short distance upstream. In summer there is a tea shop here. The weir is popular with kayakers , as the open gates generate various waves.

❷ Built in the 12th century as a guest house for the nearby Priory, the Olde Bell is one of the oldest inns in England. For hundreds of years a sanctus bell was rung to signal to the monks that an important visitor had arrived and this bell still hangs by the porch. Famous guests have included Winston Churchill and General Eisenhower, visiting the nearby US intelligence station before the D Day landings of WW2.

❸ Flint-faced St Mary's is the nave of Hurley Priory, consecrated in 1086 as the Benedictine Monastery of Our Lady. The Priory was dissolved by Henry VIII in 1536 and the remains now centre on the church, with the original cloisters and dormitories identified by blocked up windows and doors. Among its treasures are a late 14th century font, an early 17th century monument to the Lovelace family and a Saxon wooden cross, high up on the east wall. Nearby are an enormous 13th century tithe barn (now Tithecote Manor) and dovecote, showing the wealth of the Priory.

St Mary's Church

Blue Plaque at Hurley Manor

The Olde Bell

WALK SIX : PANGBOURNE

A stroll through water meadows by a reach of the river with links to *The Wind in the Willows* and *Three Men in a Boat*.

START/PARKING: Pangbourne Recreation Ground car park (free) on the left at the end of Thames Avenue off B471 Whitchurch Road, Pangbourne (Nat Grid Ref 41/637767, Postcode RG8 7BU). Alternative pay and display parking nearby at the River Meadow and Pangbourne Club car parks
PUBLIC TRANSPORT: Pangbourne rail station, about ¼ mile from start; Thames Travel bus 143 from Reading, Mon - Sat
DISTANCE: 2 miles (3¼ km)
REFRESHMENTS: The Swan pub (www.swanpangbourne.co.uk) and several cafes and pubs and a Co-op store in the village centre
PUBLIC TOILETS: Recreation Ground car park (8am to 6pm April to September) and at the Village Hall car park in Station Road, Pangbourne
PATHS: Level footpaths and meadow, liable to be muddy after wet weather (and may be flooded when the Thames is high)
CHILDREN'S PLAYGROUND: Recreation Ground

THE ROUTE: The large recreation ground has a well-equipped children's playground suitable for primary and pre-school children. From here, head across Pangbourne Meadow ❶ towards the attractive Whitchurch Bridge ❷. There are several benches here from which to watch any river activity - pleasure boats, canoes and waterfowl – and plenty of space for picnics. Turn right to follow the Thames Path across the grass, passing boat moorings and a National Trust sign before crossing a wooden bridge. After this, bear slightly right across another meadow along a path that soon follows a field boundary. There are wide views ahead and to the left of the wooded Chilterns on the other side of the Thames and the song of soaring skylarks is often heard here!

After crossing a small concrete bridge over a brook, bear left to join a path heading back towards the Thames. At the river, turn left through a gate and cross a small bridge over the brook to a boardwalk over marshy ground. The path then leads to the bridge back into Pangbourne Meadow. Follow the riverside path towards the end of Whitchurch Bridge and leave the meadow through a metal gate.

After passing the Adventure Dolphin centre on the left, carefully cross Whitchurch Road to the footpath opposite, by a brick wall. Follow this path across a stony track (Ferry Lane) to a small riverside garden looking across to a weir. There are benches here to sit and admire the lovely view. The path continues on a bridge over the River Pang towards Pangbourne station. At the road, turn right along the pavement to the Swan pub ❸, in a stunning riverside setting by the weir. From here, re-trace your steps to Pangbourne Meadow and the start of the walk.

The centre of Pangbourne is well worth visiting with cafes, pubs and a good range of shops, most of them independent. Next to the parish church of St James the Less is Church Cottage where Kenneth Grahame, author of 'The Wind in the Willows', lived from 1924 until his death in 1932. In the garden of Church Cottage is the old village lock-up, a small brick building with a conical roof. This was apparently used by Grahame as a garden shed!

A walk exploring neighbouring Whitchurch-on-Thames is given in *Weekend Walks West of Reading*

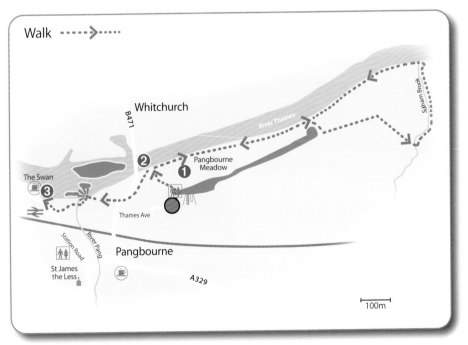

Facts and Figures

❶ Pangbourne Meadow is managed by the Parish Council and the adjacent six acres downstream by the National Trust. The reach of the Thames here and downstream is said to have been the inspiration for E H Shepard's illustrations for *The Wind in the Willows*, whose author Kenneth Grahame lived in Pangbourne.

❷ Whitchurch Bridge is one of only two toll bridges on the non-tidal Thames. The first bridge was built in 1792 and replaced in 1853. Both these were wooden and an iron one was built in 1901-02. This was rebuilt in 2013-14, retaining the attractive design.

❸ This attractive 17th century inn features in *Three Men in a Boat* as the place where the rain-soaked travellers abandoned their river adventure and caught a train back to London from the nearby station.

Thames from Pangbourne Meadow

The weir from The Swan

A ramble along a quiet stretch of river, spanned by a beautiful bridge.

START/PARKING: Wharf Road, Shillingford off the A4074 about 300m west of the Shillingford roundabout (Nat Grid Ref 41/595925, Postcode OX10 7EW), where there is roadside parking or the Shillingford Bridge Hotel (Nat Grid Ref 41/596920, Postcode OX10 8LZ) where there is a pay and display car park
PUBLIC TRANSPORT: Thames Travel buses X38/X39/X40 Oxford-Wallingford-Reading/Henley stop on the A4074 at Shillingford
DISTANCE: 1¼ miles (2 km) or 2 miles (3¼ km)
REFRESHMENTS: Shillingford Bridge Hotel (www.shillingfordbridgehotel.co.uk)
PUBLIC TOILETS: None, but toilets at the Hotel for customers
PATHS: Footpaths and a farm track; the riverside paths are liable to be muddy after wet weather (and may be flooded when the Thames is high)
CHILDREN'S PLAYGROUND: None known

THE ROUTES: There are two options, the longer route begins at Shillingford Wharf and the shorter one at the Shillingford Bridge Hotel.

At the end of Wharf Road is Shillingford Wharf, with a thatched boathouse and benches from which to admire the river. Note the historic flood levels on the wall of Swan Cottage, including those from December 1768 and January 1809 that declare "Up to this Stone the Water run". Follow the footpath by Swan Cottage, signed Thames Path, turning right along a wall and ahead at the entrance to Shillingford Court. Bear left after a gate to join a single track road and at the end of this turn right on to Shillingford Bridge ❶. Initially the footpath over the bridge is rather narrow, so care is needed. There are fine views up- and downstream from the bridge. At the end of the bridge, turn right past Shillingford Bridge Hotel.

At the far end of the Hotel car park, go down across the grass and join a path between trees. Continue ahead along this riverside path to pass over a small wooden bridge. Just beyond, where a path joins from the left, there is an information board about the Earth Trust's River of Life project ❷. Keep to the riverside path, from which views open up of Shillingford Court and the adjacent Wharf. Take the next path on the left through a metal field gate and follow this to another metal gate. Turn right here along a grassy footpath. Where this reaches a farm track, turn sharp left to join the track. This is fringed with wild flowers in the summer and leads back to the grounds of the Hotel. To reach the start at Wharf Road, re-trace your steps over the bridge and turn left to follow the Thames Path.

Facts and Figures

❶ In 1767 a centuries-old ferry was replaced by a wooden bridge, part of a new turnpike (toll road) to Reading via Wallingford. The present stone structure, with its three noble arches, was built in 1827 - one of the most beautiful bridges across the Thames. Tolls were collected on the ferry and the bridges until 1874.

❷ The Earth Trust is based at nearby Little Wittenham. Its River of Life project aims to establish new wetland habitats along 1½ miles of the south bank of the Thames here (www.earthtrust.org.uk).

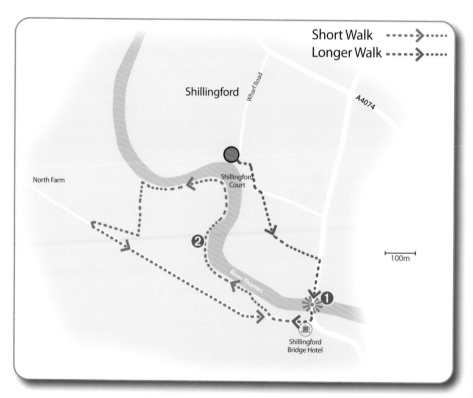

Shillingford Bridge

The Wharf

Wharf Flood Level Stone

Summer Wild Flowers

Field Bindweed

Indian Balsam

Meadow Cranesbill

Self Heal

25

Plenty to see on a loop along a reach busy with water-based activities.

START/PARKING: Mill Lane, Lower Shiplake off the A4155 (Nat Grid Ref 41/775788, Postcode RG9 3NA). There is roadside parking here and in nearby Mill Road. Alternative parking is usually available at weekends and BH at Shiplake station car park (free)

PUBLIC TRANSPORT: Shiplake rail station, about 400m from the route. Arriva bus route 800 Reading to Henley and High Wycombe passes along the A4155 , about 600m from the start

DISTANCE: 2 miles (3¼ km)

REFRESHMENTS: The Corner Shop (open Mon – Fri to 5.30pm and weekends to 12.30pm) and The Baskerville pub (www.thebaskerville. com), both in Station Road

PUBLIC TOILETS: Shiplake Lock (possibly re-opening) and at The Baskerville for customers

PATHS: Footpaths and village roads. The paths are liable to be muddy after wet weather and flooded when the Thames is high

CHILDREN'S PLAYGROUND: Badgers Walk, Shiplake (reached via Oaks Road, off Station Road)

THE ROUTE: From Mill Lane, a tarmac path on the right leads along a flint wall to Shiplake Lock ❶, busy with boats in the summer. Returning to Mill Lane, turn right and follow the lane until it becomes a gravel track that passes under the railway ❷. Immediately after the bridge, turn right along a path parallel to the railway. On reaching the river, turn left to join the riverside path. There are good views of the riverside properties and moorings of Wargrave on the opposite bank and usually plenty of boating activity on the water. Follow the towpath as far as a bench and an information panel about the Lashbrook Ferry.

Turn left to pass through a gate and follow the path across fields, going over a wooden bridge. After passing through a kissing gate at the field edge, the path bears left and under a (very low!) railway bridge. It then leads via a narrow lane to Mill Road. From here, Lower Shiplake village (and rail station) is about 400m to the right. To continue the walk, turn left and follow Mill Road as far as Lashbrook House, opposite Crowsley Road. Turn left along the drive here then, just after crossing a pair of brick bridges over a brook, turn right down a few steps and through a kissing gate to join a path. Follow this path across a field, through another gate then along a field edge to return to the start in Mill Lane.

"Mellowed in the drowsy sunlight of a summer's afternoon, Wargrave, nestling where the river bends, makes a sweet old picture … ", Chapter XIV of 'Three Men in a Boat' by Jerome K Jerome

A riverside walk at nearby Henley-on-Thames is given in *Weekend Walks South of Oxford*

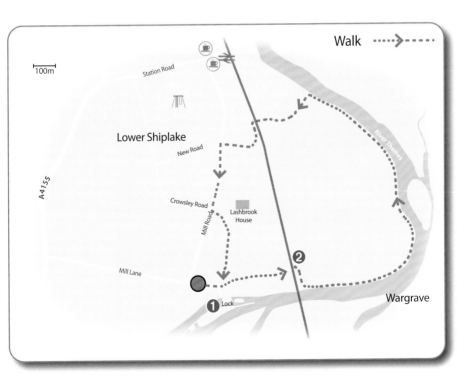

Facts and Figures

1 The first pound lock was built here in 1773, replacing a flash lock. This was next to Shiplake corn mill, mentioned in the Domesday Book. In the late 19th century, the island was bought by the City of London Corporation for camping and soon after the mill was demolished. The Thames Conservancy took over the camping island in 1914 and divided it into 18 plots, which are still leased to plot holders.

2 The branch line from Twyford to Henley-on-Thames was opened by the Great Western Railway in 1857. Popular with commuters and visitors, it is now known as the Regatta Line after the rowing event held each summer at Henley since 1839.

Shiplake Lock

Heading upstream past the Camping Island

Thatched house on the Wargrave bank

A ramble by the river where it passes this 'picture postcard' village.

START/PARKING: Sonning Lane (B4446), off the A4 about 3 miles NE of Reading town centre, where roadside parking is usually available towards the village (Nat Grid Ref 41/755755, Postcode RG4 6ST)

PUBLIC TRANSPORT: Thames Valley bus routes 127/128/129 Reading to Maidenhead /Wokingham, Mon-Sat

DISTANCE: 2 miles (3¼ km)

REFRESHMENTS: The Bull Inn (www.bullinnsonning.co.uk); The Village Hamper, High St; Coppa Club by Sonning Bridge; Tea Garden at Sonning Lock (summer months)

PUBLIC TOILETS: Sonning Lock and toilets at the Bull and the Coppa Club for customers

PATHS: Pavements, farm tracks and footpaths; some paths liable to be muddy after wet weather (and flooded when the Thames is very high)

CHILDREN'S PLAYGROUND: King George V Field, Liguge Way off Pound Lane Sonning (RG4 6XD), about 300m from the route

THE ROUTE: From the entrance to Bishops Close at the village end of Sonning Lane, walk ahead along Pearson Road. This has many fine houses and pretty cottages, including the Robert Palmer almshouses on the left and the Village Hall (named after Hugh Pearson, a 19th century vicar of Sonning). Shortly after crossing Pound Lane, at the mini-roundabout turn right into Charvil Lane. After about 250m, at the entrance to Reading University's Sonning Farm, carefully cross the road and go through a gate to join a farm track (permissive path). Follow this track (Broadmoor Lane) as glorious views over the Thames Valley open up. After about 300m, another farm track (with an 'aquatic research' signpost) leads off to the left*. Turn left along this permissive path and continue ahead to pass through gates and along a grassy farm track that becomes a footpath at the edge of a meadow. At a kissing gate at the end, turn left to join the riverside path.

The path leads past Sonning Court ❶ and moorings to the lawns of the Great House Hotel by Sonning Bridge ❷. The grassy area in front of the hotel, known as the Wharf, has benches to pause and take in the riverside scene. From here, go under the bridge (or cross the road if the river is high) and continue along the tarmac riverside path to reach picturesque Sonning Lock ❸. There are benches here from which to admire the gardens and watch folk 'messing about in boats' in spring and summer. Then re-trace your steps as far as a footpath on the right that leads to St Andrew's church ❹. An arch in the brick wall to the right leads to a peaceful garden and a gate ahead leads to the Bull Inn. After passing the inn, turn right into High Street then right again into Pearson Road and the start of the walk.

For a longer route, about 1½ miles extra, continue ahead along the Broadmoor Lane track to pass some farm buildings on the right. Where the track bears left, continue ahead along a grassy track, with a hedgerow to the right. At the corner of the field, go through a kissing gate into a narrow lane (Milestone Avenue). Turn left here and follow the lane to a bridge over St Patrick's Stream – a good place to play 'pooh sticks'! Don't cross this bridge but turn left to join the riverside path back towards Sonning.

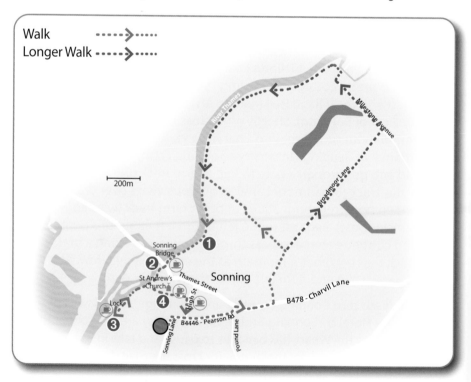

".... the most fairy-like little nook on the whole river....more like a stage village than one built of bricks and mortar", Jerome K Jerome describing Sonning in Chapter XIV of 'Three Men in a Boat'

Facts and Figures

❶ The spoon-bending illusionist Uri Geller lived at Sonning Court for 35 years until 2015.

❷ Sonning Bridge with 10 brick arches was built in 1775. Better suited to the pedestrians and pack animals it was intended for, it now carries large volumes of road traffic. It leads to Sonning Mill, converted to a Dinner Theatre in 1969.

❸ The first pound lock here was constructed in 1773 and re-built three times since. There is a tea garden on the lock island from April to October.

❹ St Andrew's church was founded in Saxon times but largely rebuilt in the mid-19th century. It has very fine memorial brasses and monuments. The former Prime Minister Theresa May is a Sonning resident and regularly worships here. The 16th century timber-framed Bull Inn next door was originally called Church House, a guest house for pilgrims, and is still owned by the church.

St Andrew's Church

Sonning Lock

Discover this stunning stretch of the Thames as it flows though the Goring Gap between the Berkshire Downs and the Chilterns.

START/PARKING: Car park at Streatley Recreation Ground, a short distance down a lane signed 'Cleeve Court' off the A329 about 150m north of the junction with the A417 (Nat Grid Ref 41/593812, Postcode RG8 9LJ)

PUBLIC TRANSPORT: Goring and Streatley rail station, about ¼ mile from Goring bridge. Going Forward buses from Wallingford to Goring, Mon - Fri

DISTANCE: 2 miles (3¼ km)

REFRESHMENTS: The Bull Inn, Streatley by the A329/B4009 crossroads with car park at rear (www.bullinnpub.co.uk); Coppa Club, Streatley (www.coppaclub.co.uk); Village Café (open daily); Pierreponts Café near Goring bridge (www.pierreponts.co.uk) and several pubs in Goring

PUBLIC TOILETS: Wheel Orchard car park, Goring. Toilets at the Bull Inn and Coppa Club for customers

PATHS: Level footpaths and pavements; the riverside paths are liable to be muddy after wet weather (and may be flooded when the Thames is high)

CHILDREN'S PLAYGROUND: Recreation Ground

THE ROUTE: The attractive tree-fringed Recreation Ground has a playground suitable for primary and pre-school children, an 'outdoor gym', benches and plenty of space for a picnic. In the corner near the car park is the entrance to the 'Wild Wood' ❶, an interactive nature discovery area well worth exploring.

To begin the walk, from the playground follow the path along the lower part of the Recreation Ground to the corner. Shortly after leaving the Recreation Ground, opposite Streatley STW, turn left through a gate to join a footpath across a field. At the gate on the other side of the field, go ahead along a boardwalk. This path leads to another gate and the Thames, with views of nearby Goring Bridge and Goring Lock. Follow the riverside path to the left, with views across to riverside homes and boathouses on the opposite bank. A steep footbridge crosses an inlet with moorings for Cleeve Court and shortly after, a gate leads to a single track road. There is plenty of space for riverside picnics and Cleeve Lock lies a short distance ahead, with a small garden from which to watch any boating activity.

To continue the walk, re-trace your steps along the riverside path; towards Streatley there are views of the hills to the south-west including nearby Lardon Chase (138m), part of the Berkshire Downs and managed by the National Trust. Turning away from the river, pass through the gate to re-join the boardwalk. At the corner where this turns left, the path back towards the Recreation Ground is through the gate to the right.

To explore more of Streatley (and Goring), continue along the boardwalk and at the end turn left to join a narrow lane past St Mary's parish church ❷. This leads to the High Street, and turning left here soon leads to the Swan Hotel and the Coppa Club, on the left by the start of Goring Bridge ❸. From the bridge there are glorious views of the river including the weir, Goring Lock and an Oxford barge that belonged to Magdalen College moored upstream of the Swan. At the Goring end of the bridge is Pierreponts Café, and access to Goring Lock. To visit this, carefully cross the road and turn right to follow the path past Goring Mill to the river; the lock is under the bridge to the right.

To complete the walk, return to Streatley over the bridge and turn right into Church Lane. Where the footpath signed 'To the River' leaves to the right, continue slightly left along a track that leads back to the Recreation Ground.

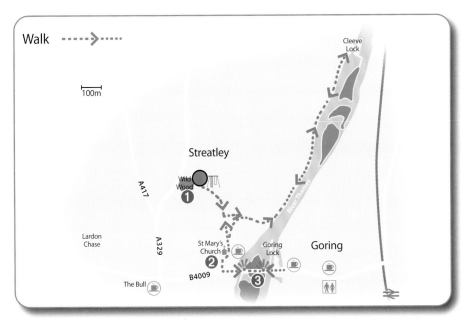

"… the sweet smiling face of the river here lured us to linger for a while; and so we left our boat at the bridge, and went up into Streatley, and lunched at the Bull …", Chapter XVI of 'Three Men in a Boat' by Jerome K Jerome

A walk exploring more of Goring-on-Thames is given in *Weekend Walks West of Reading*

Facts and Figures

❶ The Wild Wood has a nature trail to find 10 hidden (QR) codes that give information about the plants and animals that live there and set challenges – all in a fun way that will appeal to families especially. It was set up by the Heart of Streatley Charitable Trust (www.streatleywildwood.co.uk).

❷ There has been a church on this site since Saxon or even earlier times. The present building results from extensive restoration in the mid-19th century, when additions were made to the 15th century tower. A blue plaque recalls that Lewis Carroll, author of *Alice in Wonderland*, preached here (www.st-marys-streatley.org.uk).

❸ Before a toll bridge was built in 1837, the river crossing was by boat from Ferry Lane. The present bridge was built in 1923 when tolls were abolished. On 3 June 2012 the bridge was the venue of the largest street party in the UK, attended by over 4000 people and stretching for over half a mile.

St Mary's Church

Goring Lock

From a 'new' navigation, past the foaming weirs and tranquil pools of the old river course, to this attractive village.

START/PARKING: Culham Lock car park (free) at the northern end of Sutton Bridge, off the A415 about 1½ miles SE of Abingdon (Nat Grid Ref 41/509950, Postcode OX14 4NE)
PUBLIC TRANSPORT: Thames Travel bus route 33 from Abingdon to Didcot and Wallingford (Mon – Sat)
DISTANCE: 1¾ miles (2¾ km)
REFRESHMENTS: George and Dragon and The Swan pubs, Sutton Courtenay; kiosk at Culham Lock on summer weekends
PUBLIC TOILETS: None, but toilets at the pubs for customers
PATHS: Footpaths, pavements and a farm track
CHILDREN'S PLAYGROUND: Sutton Courtenay Recreation Ground, Old Wallingford Way (OX14 4AR), about 600m south of All Saints' Church

THE ROUTE: To begin the walk, go through a gate on the right near the car park entrance and turn right to join the path along Culham Cut ❶. There are several benches here and an information panel about Culham Lock. Continue past the Lock along the path by the Cut, as far as a footbridge. After crossing this bridge, bear right to join a stony farm track. This leads to a path that passes the building of a new hydro-power scheme ❷ then goes over a bridge by a weir. The path then follows an old causeway through woods, crossing three smaller weirs and passing the picturesque Sutton Pools on the left. Moorings and boathouses complete the tranquil riverside scene. At the site of an old mill, the path swings right to cross the millstream on a footbridge and leads to the end of Church Street in Sutton Courtenay.

After carefully crossing the road at the bend, follow the (uneven) pavement to the right past a row of pretty cottages. This then leads past the George and Dragon pub and the beautiful parish church ❸ to the attractive village green, with a war memorial and The Swan pub. The church and churchyard are well worth visiting. From the green, a path next to the churchyard's wall leads to it and to All Saints Lane on the far side. Turn left here and follow this to Appleford Road, by The Fish restaurant/bar, then carefully cross the road into the driveway directly opposite (private road). Near the end of this, a stile leads into a meadow. Follow the path along the field edge to reach the river, with views of nearby Sutton Bridge, to a gate to the road. Beware traffic here - great care is needed to cross to the pavement on the opposite side. Turn left and go over the bridges over the Thames then the Cut to return to the start.

"They are picturesque little spots these locks.......You meet other boats there, and river gossip is exchanged", Chapter XVIII of 'Three Men in a Boat' by Jerome K Jerome

A walk exploring the riverside and historic buildings of nearby Abingdon is given in *Weekend Walks South of Oxford*

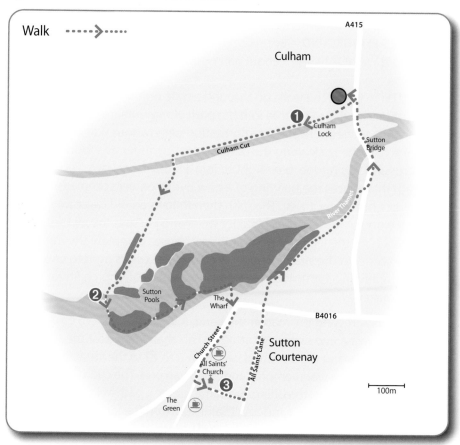

Facts and Figures

❶ This ¾ mile long navigation was built in 1809 to by-pass a difficult stretch of the Thames past a watermill at Sutton Courtenay. At the same time, Sutton Bridge was extended and Culham Lock was built – one of the deepest on the river, with a fall of nearly eight feet.

❷ The Culham hydropower scheme comprises three large Archimedes screw turbines, with passes for fish and eels. The 400 KW of green energy it can generate is used locally or exported to the National Grid.

❸ All Saints' parish church dates from the 12th to 16th centuries. The west tower has a clock with a one-handed dial and by the tower door are crosses said to have been carved by soldiers returning from the Crusades, giving thanks for their safe return. The churchyard includes the graves of the author George Orwell, best known for *Animal Farm* and *1984*, and Herbert Asquith, Prime Minister 1908-16 whose country home was The Wharf in Church Street. Orwell's simple grave is towards the SE corner of the churchyard (marked with his real name Eric Arthur Blair) and H H Asquith's large stone tomb is near the centre.

Down River to Lock and bridge

Sutton Bridge

All Saints Church

12

WALK TWELVE : WALLINGFORD

Riverside rambles from an ancient bridge to a modern one, passing historic churches and a nature reserve.

START/PARKING: Car park at the Riverside Park, reached via Stephen's Field near the eastern end of Wallingford Bridge (Nat Grid Ref 41/611895, Postcode OX10 8EB). This pay and display car park is free after 3pm on Saturday and all day Sunday

PUBLIC TRANSPORT: Thames Travel buses from Reading, Oxford, Didcot and Henley.

DISTANCE: 1½ miles (2½ km) or 2¼ miles (3½ km)

REFRESHMENTS: Café at Riverside Park when the pool is open (summer); The Boat House pub by the river and various cafés, pubs and shops in Wallingford

PUBLIC TOILETS: Riverside Park (April – Sept) and at car parks in Wallingford

PATHS: Riverside footpaths, liable to be muddy after wet weather (and flooded when the Thames is high), bridleways and pavements

CHILDREN'S PLAYGROUND: Crowmarsh Gifford Recreation Ground, Bellamy Way (reached from the car park via a footpath off Stephen's Field) and Bull Croft, off High Street Wallingford (west of town centre crossroads)

THE ROUTES: The Riverside Park has plenty of space for picnics, a children's water play area and an open air swimming pool (summer). There are good views of the river and Wallingford on the opposite bank, and an information panel.

To begin the walks, go under the arch of Wallingford Bridge ❶ nearest the river. Just beyond, there is an information panel about the Riverside Meadows. Follow the riverside path for about 500m over two footbridges and through several kissing gates. A variety of interesting buildings line the opposite bank, the last of which is the large, modern Oxford University Boat Club. Just beyond this, before a fence, turn left across the grass along a path towards farm buildings. At a footpath sign by a fence, turn right to pass through a metal kissing gate. Continue into the yard of Newnham Farm, keeping left, and leave the farmyard through a metal farm gate on your left. Then immediately bear right on to a narrow road that shortly leads to the little flint church of St Mary's, Newnham Murren ❷ through a gate on the right. There is an information board in the porch. Continue through a gate along a path that leads past the recently established

Watermead Nature Reserve on the right. There is a plan of this by each entrance gate, showing a path that leads down to the river.

For the shorter route, avoiding a busy road bridge, see * on page 40.

Just before the Wallingford by-pass, take a path on the right to go up to Winterbrook Bridge. After crossing the bridge (care is needed as the road can be busy), turn right down a tarmac path to the river. Bear left here to join the riverside path, which becomes shady with glorious open views of the opposite bank. The path leads to the Oxford University Boat Club seen previously, then narrows before emerging in a narrow road (Lower Wharf). On the right, by The Salt House, a narrow path leads through an archway under a house and over a footbridge. The churchyard of St Leonard's ❸

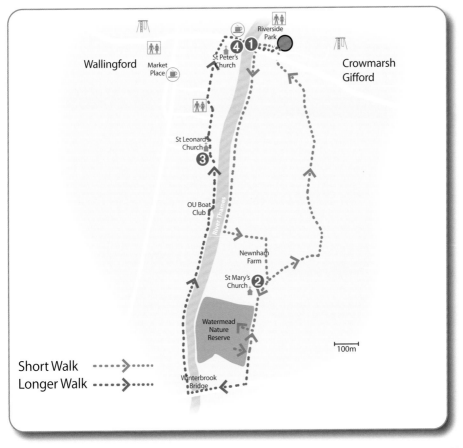

is on the left, with an information panel about this ancient building. At the corner of the road here, turn right into Thames Street which leads past the gateway to Castle Priory and along its long wall, made with an extraordinary mixture of materials. Wallingford town centre, with its attractive Market Place, cafés, pubs and shops, is nearby via turnings to the left. On the right near the end of Thames Street is St Peter's church with its attractive open work spire ❹. Turn right here and carefully cross the road by the Boat House pub, before crossing the bridge to return to Riverside Park.

* For the shorter route, re-trace your steps from Watermead along the path and road past St Mary's church, Newnham Farm and houses on the left. At a corner where the road bears right, take a bridleway on the left between fields. At a path crossroads near some houses, continue along the bridleway ahead. Where this bears right, take the path ahead across a field towards Wallingford Bridge and the start of the walk.

Facts and Figures

❶ When William the Conqueror and his army crossed the Thames here in 1066 before marching on London, they used a ford and, presumably, boats. A bridge was first recorded in 1141. The present one dates from the early 1800s and is about 300m long with 19 arches.

❷ The charming St Mary's church dates back to the early 12th century and its Norman origins can be seen in the north doorway and chancel arch. A new bell cote was added during restoration in 1849. It is now redundant and cared for by the Churches Conservation Trust.

❸ St Leonard's is the oldest church in Wallingford, dating back to the late Saxon period. Saxon stonework, laid in a herringbone pattern, is most easily seen in the north wall and over the round-headed windows. The church was damaged in the English Civil War during the 1646 Siege of Wallingford, and repaired later in the 1600s. When rebuilt in the 19th century, fortunately sections of the Saxon building were preserved.

❹ The original medieval St Peter's was destroyed by Parliamentary forces in 1646 during the Siege of Wallingford. The church was re-built 1763-69 and the distinctive spire was added in 1770. These dates may be seen carved in stone below the spire.

"Wallingford …. Is a very ancient town, and has been an active centre for the making of English history", Chapter XVIII of 'Three Men in a Boat' by Jerome K Jerome

Walks exploring more of historic Wallingford - the Castle and Saxon earthworks – are given in *Weekend Walks South of Oxford*

Wallingford Bridge and St Peter's Church from Riverside Park

Thames path sign

St Mary's Church, Newnham Murren

Further Information

Some useful websites to help you plan and enjoy the walks.

MET OFFICE
www.metoffice.gov.uk
Local weather forecasts for 1 to 5 days ahead.

ORDNANCE SURVEY
www.ordnancesurvey.co.uk
Mapping services, including online access to Landranger and Pathfinder maps.

ARRIVA BUSES
www.arrivabus.co.uk
Maps and timetables for buses in East Berkshire and South Oxfordshire.

THAMES VALLEY BUSES
www.thamesvalleybuses.com
Maps and timetables for buses in East Berkshire.

THAMES TRAVEL BUSES
www.thames-travel.co.uk/timetables-fares/
Maps and timetables for buses in South Oxfordshire.

GOING FORWARD BUSES
www.goingforwardbuses.com
Bus timetables for South Oxfordshire.

GREAT WESTERN RAILWAY TRAINS
www.gwr.com
Timetables, tickets and train running information.

SOUTH OXFORDSHIRE TOURISM
www.southernoxfordshire.com
Things to see and do in South Oxfordshire.

THAMES PATH
www.visitthames.co.uk and www.nationaltrail.co.uk
Information about the long distance walking trail.

BERKSHIRE RECORD OFFICE
www.berkshirerecordoffice.org.uk
Historical information about the Thames Conservancy and the Thames Path.

GEOCACHING
www.geocaching.com
Treasure hunting using a GPS receiver to seek hidden small containers with logbook and items such as toys and trinkets. There are 'geocaches' on or close to all the walks.

By the same author

Weekend Walks West of Reading

Twelve short walks in the Thames and Kennet valleys and Berkshire
Downs, within the triangle Reading – Newbury – Didcot

Updated and reprinted in 2017

ISBN 978-0-9929688-1-6

Weekend Walks South of Oxford

Twelve short walks in the Chilterns, the Vale and by the Thames,
within the triangle Oxford – Wantage – Henley

Updated and reprinted in 2021

ISBN 978-0-9929688-4-7

Short Scenic Strolls For All Ages
in West Berks and South Oxon

Short Scenic Strolls For All Ages
in South Oxfordshire

Weekend Walks by the Thames

Twelve short, circular, scenic walks
along the Berkshire and Oxfordshire
reaches of the River Thames. None is more
than 3 miles long.

The routes are perfect for anyone keen to explore the riverside villages and
towpaths of the picturesque middle Thames, but who don't want to walk
too far. They will suit those wanting exercise for an hour or two seeing great
scenery and interesting sights, including families with children. They are
mainly level and along public footpaths or pavements.

Each walk includes places of interest and a café, pub or shop and several
have a playground for any children taking part. Information is given
about the starting point, the route to follow and sights along the way.
See spectacular views, locks busy with boats, foaming weirs and historic
buildings – including one of the oldest pubs in England!

John Prior has lived locally for over 40 years. These walks are family
favourites – providing exercise by the river that inspired those classic books
The Wind in the Willows and *Three Men in a Boat*.

ISBN 978-0-9929688-3-0

£ 5.95

9 780992 968830